THE BEAVER

To Sam M.L.

To Laurens D.N.

Text copyright © 1981 by Margaret Lane
Pictures copyright © 1981 by David Nockels
All rights reserved.
Library of Congress Catalog Card Number: 81-67074
Printed in Italy.
First Pied Piper Printing 1983
A Pied Piper Book is a registered trademark of The Dial Press.
First published in Great Britain in 1981 by Methuen/Walker Books

THE BEAVER is published in a hardcover edition by The Dial Press,
1 Dag Hammarskjold Plaza, New York, New York 10017.
ISBN 0-8037-0637-5

THE BEAVER

By Margaret Lane

Pictures by
David Nockels

THE DIAL PRESS/New York

a pied piper book

Beavers build their own houses. They live among woods and streams, mainly in countries with cold climates. A pair of beavers will choose a place on the bank of a small river and start building a dam across it. This makes the river spread out into a deep pond so that the entrance to their home will be under water, safe from enemies.

To start building, the beavers cut
down small trees with their sharp yellow
teeth. They chop the trees into logs and
branches, then drag these to the
riverbank, along with stones to weigh
the logs down and lumps of mud to stick
them together. Beavers walk on their
hind feet and carry everything in their
front paws, not on their flat
tails as people used to
believe.

This is very hard work, but beavers are strong and have thick fur coats to keep them warm and protect them in cold water. They are skilled swimmers, as much at home in water as they are on land. Their scaly tails are like rudders, and their hind feet have webs between the toes. When they are under water, they can hold their breaths for five minutes or more.

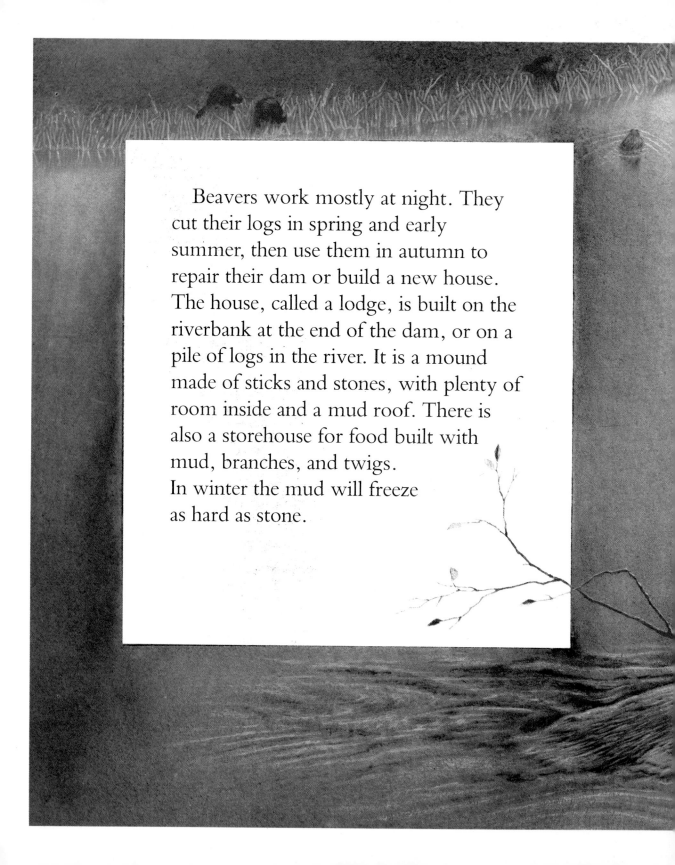

Beavers work mostly at night. They cut their logs in spring and early summer, then use them in autumn to repair their dam or build a new house. The house, called a lodge, is built on the riverbank at the end of the dam, or on a pile of logs in the river. It is a mound made of sticks and stones, with plenty of room inside and a mud roof. There is also a storehouse for food built with mud, branches, and twigs.
In winter the mud will freeze as hard as stone.

Beavers leave tiny cracks and holes in the roofs of their houses to let in fresh air. Then they dig a hole through the floor and scoop out tunnels that open deep under water. They are dedicated to their work. A pet beaver, living with a human family, will build a dam across a room with clothing, shoes, books, or anything else it can find. It makes no difference that there's not a river. When beavers hear the sound of running water—even if it comes from a faucet—they will start building.

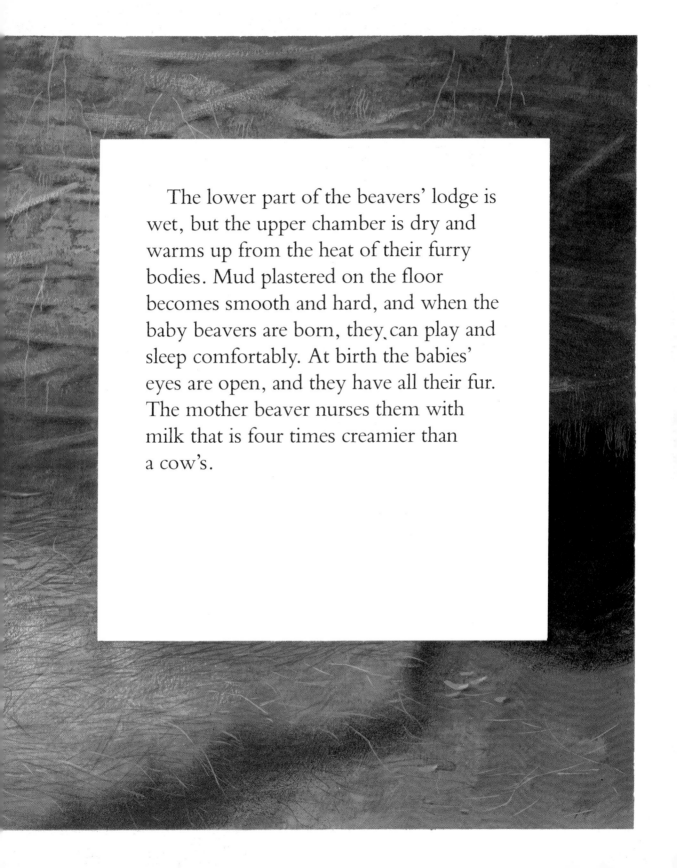

The lower part of the beavers' lodge is wet, but the upper chamber is dry and warms up from the heat of their furry bodies. Mud plastered on the floor becomes smooth and hard, and when the baby beavers are born, they can play and sleep comfortably. At birth the babies' eyes are open, and they have all their fur. The mother beaver nurses them with milk that is four times creamier than a cow's.

Baby beavers can swim when they are only four days old, and in two months their teeth are strong enough to eat the same food as their parents. Though they live on rivers and ponds, beavers do not eat fish. They feed on bark and twigs, grass, nettles, and the roots of water plants. One of their favorite foods is water lilies.

Beavers comb and clean their fur with their claws and teeth, and members of the same family will groom each other. In a pocket under their tails they have a pouch of a musky-smelling substance called castor, which they use to leave scent marks around their territory. This has long been collected by people and is an ingredient in perfumes.

Beavers live for as long as twenty years, and after a male and female first mate, they stay together for life. The young beavers live with their parents until they are two years old. When spring comes, they begin to explore, looking for a place to start building and breeding on their own. If they are slow to leave, their parents push them out of the lodge to make room for new litters of babies.

The beaver's greatest enemies are wolves and sometimes bears. Foxes and lynxes, too, roam hungrily in winter. Beavers are safe inside their lodges, but out in the woods, searching for food, they are in danger. Some dig tunnels or burrows to hide in when an enemy is near. If they smell danger when they are swimming, they whack the water with their tails to scare off the enemy and alert other beavers.

Beavers were once common in North America, Europe, and Asia, but for hundreds of years they have been hunted by people. Indians ate their meat, used their fur, and made chisels and knives from their sharp teeth. Later, trappers and hunters got high prices for beaver skins because felt made from the fur was in demand for men's top hats. Even today people still wear beaver hats, collars, and coats.

A hundred years ago beavers had
almost disappeared, but they have been
slowly multiplying, and at last people are
beginning to leave them in peace. In the
woods of Canada and much of the
United States, in Norway, Sweden, and
Russia, beavers are building their dams
again. Their lodges, as always, are their
best defense, especially in winter. So
beavers are now safe and well, at home
in the ice and snow and working as
hard as ever.

About the Author

Margaret Lane is the celebrated author of outstanding books of fiction and biography, including *A Night at Sea, A Smell of Burning,* and *The Magic Life of Beatrix Potter.* Her most recent books for young readers are *The Frog* and *The Squirrel* (both Dial). She has worked as a journalist in London and New York and has written for numerous literary publications.

Ms. Lane was educated at St. Stephen's College in Folkestone, England, and St. Hugh's College, Oxford. She lives with her husband, the 15th Earl of Huntingdon, in Beaulieu, England.

About the Artist

David Nockels is a leading illustrator in the field of natural history. Most recently he illustrated Dial's four Animal Pop-Up Books.

Mr. Nockels lives in London with his wife and son.